When an office, or a store, or perhaps your classroom, is very, very busy — people say it is a "beehive of activity."

So you can imagine how
busy it is inside a beehive.
Especially in summer.

Rookie Read-About® Science

Busy, Buzzy Bees

By Allan Fowler

Consultants

Robert L. Hillerich, Professor Emeritus,
Bowling Green State University, Bowling Green, Ohio;
Consultant, Pinellas County Schools, Florida

Scott Camazine, Ph.D, M.D., Department of Entomology,
The Pennsylvania State University

Lynne Kepler, Educational Consultant

Fay Robinson, Child Development Specialist

CHILDRENS PRESS®
CHICAGO

Design by Herman Adler Design Group
Photo Research by Feldman & Associates, Inc.

Library of Congress Cataloging-in-Publication Data

Fowler, Allan.
    Busy, buzzy bees / by Allan Fowler.
        p. cm. – (Rookie read-about science)
    ISBN 0-516-06037-6
        1. Honeybee—Juvenile literature. 2. Bees—Juvenile literature
    [1. Honeybee. 2. Bees.] I. Title. II. Series.
QL568.A6F535   1995
595.79'9–dc20   95-5557
                                                                    CIP
                                                                    AC

A hive is like a city of honeybees.

Each hive has one queen bee . . .

several hundred drones . . .

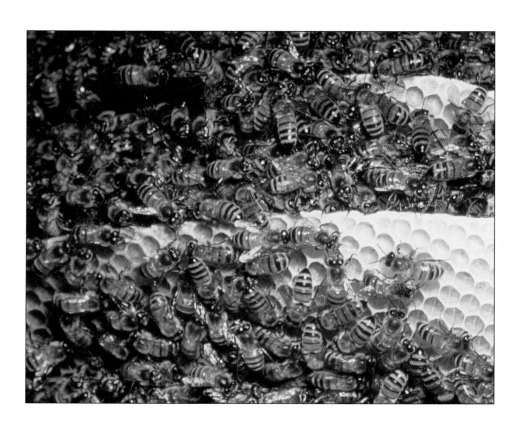

and as many as 50,000
worker bees.

The queen lives three or four years. She mates just once with the drones, or male bees.

After that, all she does is lay eggs — sometimes more than a thousand a day.

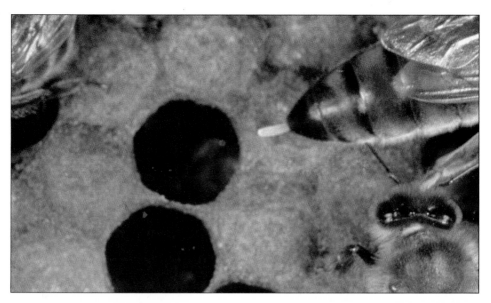

She doesn't even have to
look for food. The workers
feed her. Most worker bees
live only about six weeks,
but they certainly keep busy.

For two or three weeks, they work inside the hive. Worker bees have different jobs . . .

keeping the hive clean and
guarding it . . .

or feeding the queen and
the newly hatched larvae . . .

or adding new cells to
the honeycomb.

Worker bees build the cells
out of wax, which comes
from their own bodies.

Finally, they leave the hive and fly out into the fields to look for flowers.

Bees are attracted to blue, purple, or yellow flowers that smell sweet.

Not red ones so much, because bees can't recognize the color red.

The workers suck nectar,
a sugary liquid, from
the flowers.

While a bee is gathering
nectar, a powder called
pollen sticks to her legs
and body.

Some of it comes off when the bee visits the next flower.

By carrying pollen from one flower to another, bees help the flowers produce seeds.

New plants or flowers grow from the seeds.

The worker bees bring
the nectar back to the
food-storer bees at
the hive.

Those bees deposit it in
the cells of the honeycomb,
where it turns into honey.

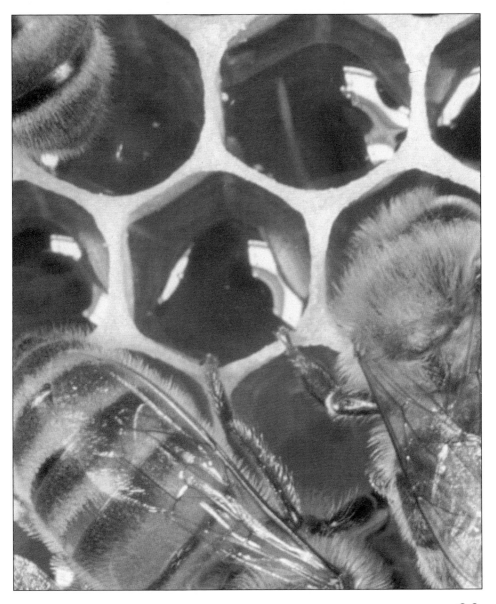

When a bee returns to the hive, she sometimes seems to start dancing.

The dance is really the bee's way of telling the other bees that she has found a good place for gathering nectar or pollen — and where that nectar or pollen is.

People known as beekeepers
set up boxes for the bees to
use as hives. The beekeepers
collect honey and wax from
the hives.

Honeybees aren't the only kind of bees. There are other bees that don't live in hives — and bees that don't sting.

But honeybees have two special gifts for us. We can thank them for giving us honey, and for helping flowers grow.

As for bee stings — no thanks!

Words You Know

honeybee

queen

drone

worker

beehive

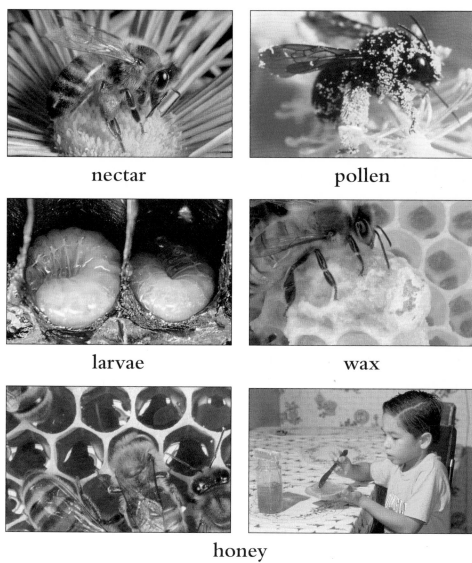

nectar

pollen

larvae

wax

honey

Index

beehives (see hives)
beekeepers, 26
bees (other than honeybees), 27
cells (of honeycomb), 14-15, 22
cleaning (of hive), 12
colors (of flowers), 16
dancing (by bees), 25
drones, 7-8, 30
eggs (of queen bee), 8
feeding (of queen bee), 10, 13
flowers, 16, 18, 21, 28
food storage (in hive), 22
hives, 3-4, 6, 11-12, 16, 22, 25-27, 30
honey, 22, 26, 28, 31
honeycombs, 14, 22, 31

larvae, 13, 31
life span (of bees), 8, 10
male bees (see drones)
mating (of bees), 8
nectar, 18-19, 22, 25, 31
pollen, 19, 21, 25, 31
queen bees, 6, 8, 10, 13, 30
seeds (of flowers), 21
smell (of flowers), 16
stings, 27-28
summer, 4
wax, 15-16, 31
winter, 5
worker bees, 7, 10-16, 18-19, 21-22, 25, 30

About the Author

Allan Fowler is a free-lance writer with a background in advertising. Born in New York, he lives in Chicago now and enjoys traveling.

Photo Credits